Original title:
Arctic Glow

Copyright © 2024 Swan Charm
All rights reserved.

Author: Liina Liblikas
ISBN HARDBACK: 978-9916-79-417-3
ISBN PAPERBACK: 978-9916-79-418-0
ISBN EBOOK: 978-9916-79-419-7

Serenade of Light on Icy Waves

In the hush of dawn's embrace,
Silver beams dance on the sea,
Whispers of old tales arise,
Carried on the breeze so free.

Glistening shards of crystal bright,
Emerge from depths of dreams untold,
Softly calling to the night,
As the day begins to unfold.

Each wave a brushstroke, pure and clear,
Painting stories in the air,
A serenade for those who hear,
Echoing a love so rare.

Reflections flicker, hearts ignite,
In the warmth of morning's gleam,
Nature's canvas, pure delight,
Cradles every heartfelt dream.

As the sun ascends the skies,
The icy waves embrace the light,
A harmony that never dies,
In the dance of day and night.

Twilight's Kiss in the Polar Realm

In the hush of dusk, shadows blend,
Whispers of night, the stars ascend.
Polar lights dance, a spectral play,
Nature's canvas, twilight's array.

Cold winds carry a secret song,
Echoes of time where dreams belong.
The auroras swirl in colors bright,
A fleeting moment, pure delight.

Celestial Glimmers on Frozen Shores

Beneath the moon, the ice does gleam,
Reflecting light like a silver stream.
Waves of starlight kiss the white sand,
In this frozen world, so grand.

Glimmers dance on the ocean's face,
Carving beauty with gentle grace.
Whispers of cosmos, calm and clear,
Here on the shore, all is near.

The Frozen Heart of Dusk

As daylight fades, shadows unfurl,
The sun whispers low, secrets swirl.
In icy breaths, the air stands still,
Frozen heart beats with nature's will.

Darkness wraps the land so tight,
Yet in the stillness, there is light.
Quiet moments, serene and bold,
Stories of dusk in silence told.

Light Play on Endless White

In fields of snow, the sun does gleam,
Painting the world with a golden dream.
Shadows stretch, long and thin,
In winter's embrace, magic begins.

Every flake, a diamond bright,
Twinkles softly in the light.
Whispers of joy in the frosty air,
Endless white is beyond compare.

Glinting Ice Flows

A river of glass, it dances and gleams,
Caught in the light, where silence redeems.
Mirrors of heaven upon the cold ground,
Whispers of winter in beauty are found.

Waves roll and swirl, with sparkles like stars,
Each crest a wonder, no grace left ajar.
Drifting like dreams on a shimmering sea,
Under the spell of the icy decree.

Immutable Beauty of White

The world is painted in shades of the pure,
Each flake a secret, each drift a allure.
Frozen stillness, a canvas unfolds,
Nature's soft lullaby, a tale to be told.

Endless horizons where white meets the sky,
Soft whispers linger as moments pass by.
In each gentle flurry, a promise remains,
The timeless embrace where silence reigns.

Nightfall's Arctic Symphony

The sun bows low, kissing ice with a sigh,
While shadows lengthen, the cold winds fly.
Crickets of frost hum their evening tune,
Under the gaze of a watchful moon.

Chords of the night weave a magical spell,
In the hushed auroras, their stories do dwell.
Notes carved in chill, in the dark they shall stay,
Echoing softly 'til the break of the day.

Chilled Luminescence

Out in the night, a glow starts to rise,
Crystals of frost like stars in the skies.
Each breath a whisper, each moment a chance,
Caught in the glow of a winter's romance.

Frosted branches dance, casting shadows so bright,
Illuminating paths in the cool of the night.
With every heartbeat, the silence expands,
Wrapped in the magic that winter commands.

Fractured Light in the Cold

In the brittle dusk, shadows fall,
Fractured light begins to crawl.
Chasing warmth from the dying day,
Echoes whisper, fade away.

Windows shimmer, edges glow,
Heartbeats quicken, spirits flow.
Beneath the frost, a flicker bright,
Hope emerges from the night.

Silhouettes dance on frozen ground,
In their movement, solace found.
Glimmers spark, a fleeting sight,
Fractured dreams take flight tonight.

Flickering Flakes

Flickering flakes in silent air,
Twirl and spin with gentle flair.
Each descent a whispered song,
Nature's rhythm, soft and strong.

Cloaked in white, the world asleep,
Secrets kept, and vows to keep.
Frosted branches, glistening bright,
Capturing moments, pure delight.

A dance of grace, a fleeting show,
Time stands still beneath the snow.
Flickering flakes in twilight's grace,
A canvas vast, a tranquil space.

The Silent Radiance

In the hush, the stars align,
The silent radiance, so divine.
Gentle beams that softly trace,
Whispers linger in boundless space.

Moonlit whispers, dreams abound,
In quietude, our hearts are found.
Each glimmer speaks, a sacred truth,
Unfolding wisdom from our youth.

The night embraces, shadows play,
In this calm, we drift away.
The silent radiance unfolds its art,
Binding souls, never apart.

Shards of Polar Brilliance

Shards of brilliance in ice confined,
Nature's splendor, intertwined.
Crystalline wonders, sharp and clear,
Echoes of winter, drawing near.

Glistening dreams in daylight's sigh,
Underneath the vast blue sky.
Zigzag patterns, endless trails,
In frozen realms where silence prevails.

Dancing colors with the sun's embrace,
Radiant sparks, a fleeting chase.
Shards of brilliance, a fleeting glance,
In this magic, hearts enhance.

Distant Starshine

In the velvet of the night,
Stars whisper tales of light.
From their heights, they send a beam,
Guiding hearts to dare and dream.

Wandering eyes behold the glow,
Secrets lost in cosmic flow.
Each twinkle sings a soft refrain,
Echoing across the vast terrain.

For every wish cast open wide,
In the universe, dreams reside.
Fleeting shadows on the ground,
In starlit silence, hope is found.

Each spark a memory's embrace,
In the dark, we find our place.
Boundless skies, we chase the light,
Distant stars, our guiding sight.

Prism of the Frozen Sky

Underneath the icy dome,
Colors twirl, the world feels home.
Reflections sparkle, shadows play,
In a dance of night and day.

Fractals weave through breaths of cold,
Stories of winter, bright and bold.
Each hue a note, a whispered song,
In the chill where hearts belong.

Glistening edges catch the light,
Painting dreams in silver-white.
With every glance, a spark ignites,
A canvas rich with frosty sights.

A prism glowing, secrets shared,
In the stillness, love is bared.
Frozen skies, forever bright,
In their embrace, we find our flight.

Glittering Snowfall

Softly falls the silent snow,
Whispers carry, gentle flow.
In the hush, the world feels new,
Blankets of white, a tranquil view.

Each flake dances from the sky,
Creating patterns, oh so nigh.
A fleeting touch upon the ground,
In this magic, peace is found.

Crystals glisten under pale light,
Transforming shadows into bright.
Winter's breath, a soothing song,
In its arms, we all belong.

In the quiet, hearts unite,
Glittering snow, pure and bright.
Nature's gift, a fleeting grace,
In the snowfall, we find our place.

Moonlit Polar Expanse

Underneath the silver glow,
Fields of ice and shadows grow.
Moonlight dances on the sea,
In the stillness, dreams run free.

An endless stretch, white and wide,
Where secrets of the night abide.
With every wave, a story calls,
Through the silence, wonder falls.

The polar night, a tranquil hymn,
Nature's canvas, vast and dim.
In the shadows, stories blend,
In the moonlit, dreams transcend.

A world adorned in icy lace,
In the cold, we find our place.
Embraced by night, the spirits soar,
In the polar expanse, we explore.

Echoes of the Icy Abyss

Whispers ride the biting breeze,
Echoes dance beneath the freeze.
Depths of silence, shadows glean,
In the stillness, frost is seen.

Caverns deep, a chilling song,
Nature's lullaby, sweet yet strong.
As the ice holds time in sway,
Secrets buried, far away.

Glimmers hint at mysteries,
Hidden 'neath the frosted trees.
Frozen echoes, history's trace,
In the depths, we find our place.

The azure depths, a portal clear,
Calling softly, drawing near.
In the void, our thoughts align,
In the icy abyss, we soon entwine.

Frosted climes, where dreams take flight,
Drifting softly through the night.
Echoes linger, calling forth,
From the depths of the frozen north.

Frost-Kissed Horizons

A blush of dawn on frosted ground,
Where silence reigns, and peace is found.
Tender whispers, earth awakes,
In the light, the stillness shakes.

Fields adorned in icy lace,
Nature dons a bright embrace.
On the edge of winter's glow,
Frost-kissed winds begin to blow.

Trees stand tall, with branches bare,
Greeting winter's frigid air.
In the morn, the world enshrines,
The beauty of these frost-kissed signs.

Colors merge, both soft and bright,
Painting scenes of pure delight.
Horizons stretched, an endless view,
Where dreams converge in crystal hue.

With each breath, the chill ignites,
Awakens warmth, invites the sights.
Frost-kissed moments, fleeting fast,
Cherish these as seasons pass.

Celestial Wintertide

Stars align in velvet skies,
Winter's charm, as daylight dies.
A dance of light, the cosmos sings,
In the hush, a peace it brings.

Snowflakes twirl like whispers light,
Blanket earth in shimmering white.
As night unfolds, the world transforms,
Embraced by winter's gentle norms.

A celestial glow, soft and clear,
Illuminates the night that's near.
Each moment holds a spark divine,
In this wintertide, hearts entwine.

The moon reflects on frosted seas,
A serenade, a gentle breeze.
In silence, dreams begin to glide,
Underneath this wintertide.

Awakening thoughts with every breath,
Fueling life, conquering death.
Celestial beauty, softly glows,
As winter's magic ever flows.

Sparkling Stillness

In the stillness, magic dwells,
Whispers wrapped in icy shells.
Crystals shine in morning light,
A world transformed, pure and bright.

Each step crunches on the snow,
Nature's blanket, soft and slow.
Frosted branches hold their breath,
In this moment, dance with death.

Stillness reigns, a sacred pause,
In the quiet, nature's laws.
Reflecting dreams in shimmering hue,
A spark of life in every view.

Beneath the weight of evening's cloak,
The world is hushed, and shadows stoke.
In the calm, intentions freed,
Sparkling stillness plants a seed.

Together we embrace the chill,
Finding warmth in nature's will.
In this moment, time stands still,
As we cherish winter's thrill.

Crystal Serenity

In silent whispers, snowflakes fall,
A gentle touch, a soft enthrall.
The world adorned in a quilt of white,
A tranquil scene, pure and bright.

Beneath the trees, a stillness reigns,
Where frozen lakes hold nature's chains.
Reflections dance on icy glass,
A fleeting moment, time will pass.

In every crystal, magic glows,
A secret charm that nature shows.
The air is crisp, the sky profound,
In this serene escape, I'm found.

As twilight falls, the stars emerge,
A cosmic song begins to surge.
The night unfolds its velvet cloak,
In whispered dreams, my heart awoke.

Glacial Serenade

Amidst the ice, a melody sings,
A harmony that winter brings.
Each breath a cloud, a fleeting sigh,
As glacial whispers meet the sky.

The mountains rise, majestic, bold,
Their stories etched in ice and cold.
The frozen winds, like secrets shared,
In nature's grasp, we are ensnared.

With every step, the crunch of snow,
A path unknown where few may go.
The beauty lingers, strong and pure,
In silence deep, our hearts endure.

As night descends, the moonlight glows,
Illuminating the path we chose.
A glacial serenade, softly played,
In this embrace, our fears allayed.

Ethereal Glow on Ice

Beneath the moon, a shimmer bright,
The ice reflects the silver light.
An ethereal glow, a magic dream,
Where time stands still, and rivers gleam.

The frosty air, alive with grace,
Nature's beauty, a soft embrace.
In every corner, wonders hide,
As frozen dreams dance side by side.

Echoes of laughter fill the night,
Children playing in pure delight.
Snowmen stand guard, a watchful cheer,
A timeless joy, with loved ones near.

As dawn approaches, colors blend,
A canvas bright, the night must end.
Yet memories linger, crisp and clear,
In ethereal glow, we hold dear.

Whispering Winds of Winter

The winds arise, a soft caress,
Whispers of winter's pure finesse.
They weave through trees, a gentle sigh,
Telling tales as they rush by.

In hushed tones, the world is hushed,
While flakes of snow begin to crushed.
A frosty breath, a touch of chill,
Nature's song, it's louder still.

The branches sway, a graceful dance,
In winter's grip, we find romance.
With every gust, a story unfolds,
In whispered winds, we are consoled.

As shadows lengthen, dusk takes hold,
The night brings warmth against the cold.
In these whispers, our hearts align,
Winter's embrace, so sweet, divine.

Ethereal Hues of the Frozen World

A whisper floats on crystal air,
Glistening in the morning light.
Blue and silver dance with flair,
Nature's canvas, pure delight.

Trees adorned with icy lace,
Every branch a work of art.
In this silent, sacred space,
Cold and warmth begin to part.

The sun dips low, a gentle glow,
Painting shadows on the snow.
In twilight's breath, the colors flow,
Ethereal beauty starts to show.

Footprints mark a wanderer's path,
Leading through this frozen dream.
Each step whispers of nature's wrath,
Yet here, it feels like a serene stream.

At dusk, the stars begin to gleam,
A tapestry of dark and light.
In this world, we dare to dream,
Ethereal hues, a wondrous sight.

Frost-Kissed Memories in Twilight

Beneath the frost, old stories lie,
Whispers of laughter, shadows cast.
In the twilight's gentle sigh,
Echoes of a vibrant past.

The world wears a cloak of white,
Softly resting on the ground.
In the fading day's last light,
Frozen moments swirl around.

A touch of frost on the windowpane,
Shapes of memories take their flight.
In coldness, warmth does remain,
Frost-kissed dreams in fading light.

Each flake a tale, a piece of time,
Swirling softly in the breeze.
In this beauty, we often climb,
To savor life's fleeting tease.

As stars awaken, shadows creep,
The night wraps the world in its arms.
In frozen stillness, we shall keep,
The warmth of our heart's deeper charms.

The Cosmic Tapestry Beyond the Snow

Above the snow, the heavens gleam,
Stars unravel, threads of gold.
In this void, we chase a dream,
The cosmic dance, ancient and bold.

Galaxies twirl, a sight divine,
Whispers of worlds once cast away.
In sparkling silence, the stars align,
Marking moments, night and day.

Through wintry bliss, we gaze in awe,
Each flake a piece of the sky's heart.
This vast expanse, a timeless law,
In every sparkle, the universe's art.

As we walk where snowflakes fall,
We reach for the celestial, the bright.
In the whispers of night, we hear the call,
Of dreams entwined in starlit flight.

Boundless beauty, a tale we weave,
In frozen realms, the cosmos sings.
In every breath, we dare to believe,
The magic that the winter brings.

Gleaming Secrets of Icebound Landscapes

In the stillness, secrets hide,
Beneath layers of crystal sheen.
Each frost-kissed wonder, nature's pride,
Hints of magic, serene and keen.

Mountains crowned with icy light,
Guardians of the whispering cold.
In their shadows, the world feels right,
As ancient tales of winter unfold.

Frozen rivers, mirrors bright,
Reflecting stories lost in time.
In their depths, the stars ignite,
Gleaming secrets in winter's rhyme.

Every crack and crevice holds,
A piece of nature's frozen lore.
In silence, the landscape unfolds,
Promising wonders to explore.

Through the chill, our hearts align,
With the rhythms of this icy land.
In each moment, a design,
Gleaming secrets, nature's hand.

Aurora's Whisper on the Frigid Sea

Beneath the stars, the ocean sighs,
A dance of hues in tranquil skies.
Cold winds speak secrets deep and low,
As auroras paint the waves aglow.

Reflections shimmer, colors twine,
The icy breath of night divine.
Each flicker tells a tale untold,
Of ancient journeys, brave and bold.

The horizon blushes, soft and bright,
As shadows cower from the light.
With whispers carried by the breeze,
The sea embraces all it sees.

In this serene and frosty trance,
The world holds still, awaits its chance.
Nature's brush strokes fill the air,
A harmony beyond compare.

The moonlight bathes the frosted ground,
While echoes of the night resound.
In chilled embrace, we find our way,
Through whispers of the night and day.

The Flicker of Light in the Winter's Grip

In winter's clutch, the shadows creep,
Yet flickers of warmth stir from sleep.
A candle glows against the frost,
A beacon bright, never lost.

The hearth's embrace, a tender glow,
While outside winds begin to blow.
Each spark ignites a dance of dreams,
As warmth spills forth in soft moonbeams.

Snowflakes twirl and weave their lace,
A fleeting moment, a frozen grace.
Through chilly nights, the light persists,
A promise held in winter's fist.

The world outside is vast and wide,
Yet here we find a place to hide.
In whispered tales, the stories spin,
Of radiant hope that lies within.

So let the cold winds howl and roar,
We've found our haven by the door.
In the flicker of light, we learn to cope,
A gentle warmth, a spark of hope.

Dances of Color Beneath Polar Skies

Beneath the skies of emerald hue,
The world awakens, fresh and new.
Whispers of jade and violet dreams,
In silent connection, nature schemes.

The icebergs float like crystal glass,
Reflecting colors as they pass.
In this ballet of light and shade,
A tapestry of night is made.

Each flicker pulls the eye to see,
The dance of colors, wild and free.
Where reds and greens in waves entwine,
A frozen canvas, pure and fine.

The stars above begin to spin,
While shadows waltz, inviting in.
With every pulse, the night ignites,
In rhythmic joy, the heart delights.

Amidst the cold, sweet warmth arises,
In nature's dance, our spirit flies.
Together, lost in this embrace,
We linger still in time and space.

Bright Shadows: A Frosty Reverie

In frosty air, where shadows play,
The world transforms in bright array.
Each corner hides a whisper soft,
A tale of frost that lifts aloft.

The morning sun spills golden rays,
Awakening the icy ways.
With every breath, the silence swells,
A gentle dance, the heart compels.

Winds wrap around in crystal threads,
While daylight chases night from beds.
In every glimmer, every glint,
The cold reveals what lies in print.

A tapestry of frigid dreams,
Where hope and wonder flow in streams.
In every shadow, secrets fold,
A frosty reverie to behold.

Together, lost in snowy peace,
Where bright shadows and beauty cease.
In winter's heart, we find our song,
An echo that will linger long.

Shimmering Silence of the North

In the stillness, snowflakes fall,
Whispers of winter, a soft call.
Moonlight dances on frozen streams,
Wrapped in nature's gentle dreams.

Trees stand tall, dressed in white,
Guardians of this tranquil night.
Footsteps echo in the deep cold,
Stories of brave hearts, bold.

Stars above twinkle with grace,
Lighting the vast, untouched space.
Every breath is a cloud of mist,
In this quiet, nothing is missed.

The world feels wrapped in a cloak,
When the howling winds softly poke.
Nature holds its breath, serene,
In the shimmering silence, so keen.

With every glance, the stillness grows,
In the north, a deeper peace flows.
Here, time pauses, a magical trance,
In the silence, we find romance.

Beneath the Polar Skies

Underneath the vast polar dome,
We find a place, a distant home.
Stars like diamonds grace the night,
A blanket of beauty, pure and bright.

Icebergs cradle the moon's soft glow,
Reflections of dreams in the snow.
Whispers travel on frosty air,
Secrets of the night, fragile and rare.

Auroras dance with vibrant hues,
Painting the sky with emerald views.
Nature's canvas, alive and bold,
Tales of adventure waiting to unfold.

When silence wraps the world in peace,
And chaotic thoughts begin to cease,
We breathe in wonders, vast and wide,
Under the polar skies, we confide.

In this realm where spirits soar,
Each breath ignites a longing for more.
In the hush of night, hearts entwine,
Beneath the polar skies, divine.

Echoes of Frozen Light

In the heart of winter's embrace,
Faint echoes linger in this place.
Crystal shards twinkle in delight,
Telling tales of frozen light.

Trees adorned with glimmering frost,
Whispers of warmth, never lost.
Footsteps crunch on the icy ground,
In this silence, magic is found.

The cold air bites, sharp and clear,
Yet in this stillness, there's no fear.
A serene beauty, haunting and bright,
Echoes of memories, day and night.

Candles flicker in window frames,
Casting shadows, calling our names.
Every glimmer tells a story,
Of winter's truth and fleeting glory.

In a world where time seems still,
Hearts awaken, a shared thrill.
Among the echoes, we take flight,
Into the realm of frozen light.

Celestial Lanterns on Snow

Celestial lanterns shine from afar,
Guiding us home like a northern star.
Each glow dances on soft white beds,
Filling our dreams, where magic spreads.

Crisp air carries soft-spoken dreams,
Where moonlit paths wind like streams.
Footsteps lead to where shadows fall,
In this serene realm, we hear the call.

The night unfolds its velvet sheet,
With wonders hidden at each heartbeat.
Nature whispers in intricate patterns,
A melody sweet that gently flatters.

Every snowflake tells a tale,
In the quiet, our spirits sail.
Together we wander, hand in hand,
Through fields of snow, oh so grand.

In the distance, a soft refrain,
Cradled in silence, we feel no pain.
Under celestial lanterns, we glow,
In the warmth of love, we overflow.

Polar Lanterns in the Deepening Chill

Lights flicker softly, a dance in the night,
Chasing shadows away from the sight.
Glowing whispers of colors so bright,
Guiding the lost with their gentle light.

Ice crystals shimmer, reflecting the glow,
A canvas adorned with nature's flow.
The whispers of winter in the cold winds blow,
Drawing hearts closer as the frost settles low.

Beneath the vast sky, silence prevails,
In the depths of night where magic sails.
With every beat, the heart unveils,
The warmth of the lanterns, a spirit that hails.

Polar dreams hold secrets untold,
In their embrace, the world feels bold.
A promise of warmth in the bitter cold,
As the lanterns glimmer, stories unfold.

Each flicker a tale spun from the past,
Of winter's embrace and how it will last.
In the stillness, memories cast,
Under polar lanterns, we'll find peace at last.

The Whispered Secrets of Icy Auroras

In the northern skies where the colors gleam,
Waltzing lights weave a shimmering dream.
Whispers of secrets in silken streams,
Painting the darkness with radiant themes.

Crimson and emerald swirl in delight,
A tender ballet through the velvet night.
Each flicker a promise, a cosmic flight,
Beneath nature's canvas, hearts feel light.

Echoes of legends float high on the breeze,
Revealing the magic with effortless ease.
In the realm of wonder, the spirit finds peace,
As the auroras dance, all worries cease.

Stars whisper softly, guiding our way,
In the realm of dreams where shadows sway.
Infinity's colors in a grand display,
Wrap us in beauty, come what may.

The night holds mysteries, a world to explore,
In the heart of winter, we seek evermore.
With every aurora, we are reborn,
In the whispered secrets, our souls will soar.

Frosted Echoes of Celestial Fire

Amidst the chill, a flicker ignites,
Dreams of warmth through the icy nights.
Frosted echoes dance, a dazzling sight,
Breath of the stars wrapped in soft light.

The cold wind carries a haunting song,
Tales of the cosmos where we belong.
In the shimmer and sparkle, we feel so strong,
Infinite moments where hearts dance along.

Celestial fire ignites the expanse,
Guiding the wanderers in their trance.
The night is alive, a cosmic romance,
Each twinkling star gives hope a chance.

Through frosted branches, whispers unveil,
The warmth of the heavens, an age-old tale.
In the depths of night, where stars set sail,
We find our purpose, in dreams we prevail.

Eternal reflections on ice's embrace,
In the frosted echoes, we find our place.
Holding the fire that time can't erase,
In the chill of the night, love leaves its trace.

Shining Beneath the Frozen Canopy

Shadows held captive beneath icy boughs,
Whispers of hope in the frosty vows.
Stars peek through layers, silent and proud,
Painting the world in a mystical shroud.

The canopy sparkles, a treasure of light,
Guiding our journeys through endless night.
Under this dome, the heart takes flight,
As dreams intertwine in a celestial sight.

Beneath winter's veil, the magic ignites,
Moments of wonder, our spirit unites.
Frozen reflections cast glowing heights,
Embracing the magic of starry delights.

A tapestry woven with shadows and dreams,
Each glimmer a promise, a thread of moonbeams.
In this quiet world, nothing's as it seems,
Under the canopy, life softly redeems.

Together we wander, hearts open wide,
Beneath the frozen canopy, side by side.
In the light of the echoes, we take our stride,
Wrapped in the warmth that the stars provide.

Surrendering to the Snowy Glow

Gentle flakes fall from the sky,
Dancing softly as they sigh.
Nature dons a pure disguise,
Underneath the silvered skies.

Footprints fade in soft descent,
Whispers of the day now spent.
Trees are draped in crystal white,
As day gives way to tranquil night.

Feel the chill beneath the stars,
Hear the silence, free of wars.
In the glow of winter's breath,
Find a peace that conquers death.

Wrapped in warmth, we stand in awe,
Of beauty that we never saw.
In this moment, time stands still,
Capturing hearts against our will.

Surrender now, let go of fears,
In this stillness, calm your tears.
For in the snow's embrace, you'll find,
A haven for your searching mind.

Celestial Choreography of Frost

Night unfurls its velvet cloak,
As the frosty tendrils soak.
Stars align in silent grace,
In this vast, enchanting space.

Crystals form on window panes,
Nature's art that still remains.
Glittering, a tale unfolds,
Of winter's touch in whispering cold.

Each breath steams in the night air,
A fleeting touch of silvered care.
The moon shines bright, a watchful eye,
As the world below breathes a sigh.

Frosty patterns twist and weave,
In delicate forms that deceive.
A ballet of nature's design,
Within the frost, pure worlds combine.

As time ebbs, this dance goes on,
In the dark, the sparks of dawn.
Celebrate this winter's show,
A celestial fairy glow.

The Icy Canvas Shines.

On the pond, the mirror gleams,
Reflecting softly all our dreams.
Brushstrokes of winter's embrace,
Painted on nature's cool face.

Underneath the frosted trees,
A whisper dances with the breeze.
Footsteps crunch on winter's art,
Each sound echoes, a pure heart.

Icicles hang like sparkling swords,
Nature's beauty hoards its rewards.
The sun pierces through icy air,
Revealing beauty everywhere.

Above, the sky a muted gray,
Yet magic lingers in the day.
With each breath, the silence flows,
In this icy canvas, we know.

Close your eyes, breathe in the chill,
Let the mirth of winter fill.
In the quiet, find your muse,
In icy strokes, let your heart choose.

Icy Whispers in the Night

Shadows stretch beneath the moon,
In the night, the world is strewn.
With icy whispers, trees confer,
Hidden tales of winter's spur.

Frosted breath hangs in the air,
Every moment laid bare.
Stars shimmer like distant dreams,
Weaving magic through moonbeams.

Crickets hush, the night feels calm,
Nature wrapped in a soothing balm.
Crystals glisten, secrets kept,
In this quiet, hearts have leapt.

Listen close, the night speaks clear,
Casting dreams, dissipating fear.
As frost blankets the tired ground,
In its promise, hope is found.

Embrace the magic, let it flow,
In winter's arms, our spirits grow.
With every icy whisper near,
We find solace, free from fear.

The Whispering Glow of Winter's Breath

In the hush of the frosty night,
Moonlight dances soft and bright,
Whispers weave through trees so bare,
Winter's breath lingers in the air.

Silent flakes begin to fall,
Covering dreams, enchanting all,
Crystal sparkles in the dawn,
Nature's beauty gently drawn.

Footprints trace the snow's soft skin,
Secrets held where we've been,
Ghostly echoes of laughter fade,
In this serene, chilly glade.

Fires flicker in windows warm,
Embers glow, a beckoning charm,
While outside, the cold wind sings,
Harmonies of the season's wings.

Stars emerge in the darkened sky,
Wonders twinkle, asking why,
In the stillness, hearts ignite,
By the whispering glow of night.

Chasing Shadows on Icy Waters

Beneath the bridge, reflections play,
Whispers caught in the light's ballet,
Glass-like surface, a mirror's gleam,
Chasing shadows, frozen dream.

Skaters glide in graceful arcs,
Painting stories with joyous sparks,
While laughter echoes, bright and clear,
In the chill, warmth draws near.

Sunset dips, the sky ablaze,
Crimson hues in twilight's haze,
As dusk descends, and whispers rise,
In the heart, a soft surprise.

Moonlit paths on a crystal lake,
Where mysteries swirl, and dreams awake,
Every ripple tells a tale,
Of fleeting moments, winds that sail.

Nature's canvas, vast and wide,
Holds the secrets that we confide,
Chasing shadows, we attempt to find,
The stories frozen, intertwined.

Light Weaving Through Wind and Snow

Golden strands of dawn's first light,
Weave through branches, pure and white,
Glistening on the fields below,
As the world begins to glow.

Wind carries tales from far away,
Whispers of night and break of day,
Snowflakes tumble in a dance,
Inviting all who dare to glance.

Each flake a story, unique and rare,
Crafted with love by the twilight air,
Together they fall, in silence they speak,
In this soft world, solace we seek.

Patterns shift with the morning's breath,
Life awakens in the shroud of death,
Colors burst through, radiant and bold,
As warmth unfolds, the tales retold.

Light weaves through, a gentle hand,
Stitching time, both vast and grand,
Embracing winter, in its soft show,
While the heart beats, steady and slow.

Illuminations of the Endless Ice

Underneath the sky so wide,
Illuminations softly glide,
On surfaces frozen, smooth and clear,
Beauty captured, winter's cheer.

Icicles hang like crystal spears,
Holding whispers of our fears,
Yet in their glow, a hope remains,
In the silence, joy sustains.

Frosted breath on every sigh,
Nature watches as time slips by,
Each moment glimmers, rich and bright,
In the embrace of endless night.

Stars like diamonds, twinkling high,
Paint the canvas of the sky,
Reflecting on the icy lakes,
In this realm, the heart awakes.

Illuminations softly fall,
Weaving magic, embracing all,
In the landscape, pure and nice,
We find our peace on endless ice.

Echoes of a Frozen Dreamscape

Whispers ride the icy breeze,
Shadows dance beneath the trees.
In silence deep, the night unfolds,
Where time stands still, and dreams are told.

Stars twinkle in the frozen air,
Ghostly visions linger there.
Fragments of a past ignite,
In the quiet of the night.

Crystals shimmer on the ground,
Ancient tales begin to sound.
Each breath a fleeting cloud of white,
Painting dreams in silver light.

Beneath a veil of endless snow,
Where only winter spirits go.
Echoes wrap around the night,
A dreamscape born from cold delight.

In slumber's grip, the world remains,
Beyond the reach of worldly chains.
A frozen realm where hopes reside,
In echoes faint, our hearts abide.

Celestial Beacons in the Snowy Void

Lights flicker in the endless night,
Celestial guardians shining bright.
Guiding lost souls through the dark,
Beneath the glow, we leave our mark.

Snowflakes dance like whispers free,
Floating on the midnight sea.
Each star a beacon glowing fair,
Illuminating paths laid bare.

In the vastness of the cold,
The ancient stories are retold.
Constellations weave their thread,
In dreams of light, we long to tread.

Celestial spheres, so far and wide,
Carry wishes on a ride.
Through the void where silence reigns,
Hope resides in cosmic lanes.

Underneath a blanket white,
We find solace in soft light.
Each twinkle serves to remind,
Of the beauty that's intertwined.

The Night's Luminous Embrace

In the hush of midnight's grace,
The shadows hold a soft embrace.
Gentle whispers, secrets shared,
In the dark, we feel prepared.

Moonlight spills like silver wine,
Telling tales of the divine.
Stars peer down with knowing eyes,
Watching dreams as they arise.

Wrapped in warmth of starlit glow,
We find peace in ebb and flow.
Each heartbeat syncs with nature's song,
As night unfolds where we belong.

Fires burn in our hearts anew,
Guiding us as we push through.
In the twilight, we awake,
Cradled in the night's soft wake.

Luminous fate in the cold air,
A promise made without a care.
In the dark, we boldly rise,
Chasing dreams beneath the skies.

A Solstice Spark in the Polar Night

A spark ignites in the polar flow,
Where sunlight fades and shadows grow.
Winter's kiss brings dreams so bright,
In the depths of a starry night.

Solstice whispers in the chill,
Time suspended, hearts stand still.
Miracles born in icy breath,
Dance with joy in the face of death.

Fires of hope in the blackened skies,
Awakening wonder, the spirit flies.
In this realm where shadows dwell,
Magic weaves its sacred spell.

Crimson hues break through the white,
A tapestry of dusk and light.
With each flicker, courage wakes,
As silence holds the world that breaks.

In this night so vast and deep,
Promises made, we vow to keep.
A spark, a glow in the endless night,
Guides us towards the morning light.

Luminescent Hues of the Frigid Expanse

In the stillness where shadows dance,
Whispers of colors start to prance.
A palette bright on a snowy plain,
Illuminating the winter's reign.

Crimson glows in the frozen air,
Emerald echoes, a jewel rare.
Sapphire sparks break the silent night,
Each hue sings of the cold's delight.

Frosted breath paints the sky above,
In the quiet, there's warmth, there's love.
Cascading lights in a crystal dome,
Nature's art, the cold feels like home.

Waves of color, a gentle breeze,
Drifting softly among the trees.
Frigid beauty wraps the earth tight,
In luminescent hues, hearts ignite.

With every twinkle, laughter swirls,
In the expanse, a wonder unfurls.
The night reveals what day conceals,
In frozen moments, the spirit feels.

The Beacons in the Bitter Cold

Amidst the chill where shadows crawl,
The beacons shine, they beckon all.
Guiding lost souls through icy trails,
Their warmth endures where the heart prevails.

Fires flicker beneath the moon,
Echoes of hope in a haunting tune.
In the bitter night, they stand tall,
A testament that love conquers all.

Each flame whispers stories untold,
Of journeys brave, of hearts bold.
In the darkness, they twinkle bright,
Reminders that warmth lives in the night.

With every gust of the winter's breath,
The beacons glow, defying death.
A signal strong in the arctic air,
In the bitter cold, we find our care.

They dance in the night, a cosmic play,
In the stillness, they find their way.
Through storm and silence, they will unfold,
The magic beneath the bitter cold.

Glimmering Dreams of the Polar Night

In a world draped in velvet skies,
Stars are sparkling, dreams arise.
Whispers of magic on the breeze,
Carried by night, they float with ease.

Silvery shadows, a silent grace,
Moonlight adorns the polar space.
Glistening dreams in the frost-clad air,
Awakening wonders beyond compare.

Each twinkle tells of fables old,
Of brave hearts, and fires bold.
In the stillness, the spirit takes flight,
On glimmering dreams of the polar night.

The auroras swirl, a dance divine,
Within the chill, secrets entwine.
A tapestry woven with stardust thread,
In the polar night, our wishes are fed.

In every heart, the dreams ignite,
Guided by stars, they shimmer bright.
A celestial canvas, vast and wide,
In glimmering dreams, we take our stride.

A Canvas of Frost and Flame

Upon the ground, a canvas laid,
Where frost and flame serenely played.
Colors clash in the winter's grasp,
In the silence, we seize and clasp.

Sparks of orange in icy streams,
Nature breathes, alive in dreams.
Each brush stroke, a story spun,
An endless dance where light has fun.

Frosty whispers, a gentle sigh,
Paint the world where shadows lie.
Flames flicker, creating delight,
Transforming the darkness into light.

With every heartbeat, a new design,
Where ice and fire gracefully align.
In the canvas of life, we find our claim,
In the merging of frost and flame.

A masterpiece formed in the heart's embrace,
Each moment captured, our sacred space.
In nature's gallery, we stake our name,
On this beautiful journey, we play the game.

Spheres of Frosty Light

Glittering orbs in the night sky,
Whispers of ice as they glide by.
Shards of silver, dreams take flight,
In the dance of the spheres of frost light.

Beneath the moon, a crystal gleam,
Nature's canvas, a fleeting dream.
Chasing shadows, soft and bright,
Boundless beauty, pure delight.

The world wrapped in a soft embrace,
Every corner a magical space.
Frosted branches, a glimmering sight,
Unveiling secrets in the pale twilight.

In silence they sing, the stars in array,
Painting the heavens, come what may.
Spheres of frost, where dreams ignite,
A cosmic lace, so rare and slight.

As dawn breaks the night's gentle hold,
The story of winter begins to unfold.
With every breath, a tale takes flight,
In the glow of the spheres, everything feels right.

Enchanted Winter Landscape

A tapestry woven, white and pure,
Snowflakes dance, their beauty sure.
Trees draped in diamonds, so divine,
An enchanted landscape, timeless shrine.

Frozen rivers, still and bright,
Mirroring dreams caught in white light.
Whispers of frost glide through the air,
Nature's secrets, a gentle prayer.

Footsteps crunch on the snowy floor,
Each step whispers of tales of yore.
In the magic of winter's embrace,
Every heartbeat finds its place.

Mountains rise like giants bold,
Wrapped in blankets of glistening gold.
A realm of wonder, in winter's sway,
Each moment breathed, a gift we lay.

As twilight descends, hues intertwine,
Painting the landscape, a sacred sign.
Lost in the beauty, a soul takes flight,
In the enchantment of this winter night.

Dusk and Dawn in the Frozen North

Where dusk kisses the frost-kissed ground,
A lullaby of stars is softly found.
In the frozen north, whispers of light,
Awakening dreams in the still of night.

Glistening shadows stretch and sway,
As night yields softly to the break of day.
The horizon blushes in golden hues,
In the dance of dusk, a silent muse.

Frosted air, crisp and clear,
Holds the silence, draws us near.
In the cradle of mountain heights,
Where echoes of winter sing through the nights.

As dawn breaks forth, the world awakes,
Every crystal spark, a heartbeat makes.
In the frozen north, time drifts and flows,
In the embrace of dusk, the spirit glows.

When twilight falls, the sky ignites,
Colors weave into wondrous sights.
In the dance of dusk and dawn's sweet breath,
Life cycles gently, defying death.

Luminescent Frostbite

In the chill of night, a glow erupts,
Luminescent frost, the world interrupts.
Crystals shimmer, kiss the ground,
A frosty magic, in silence found.

Biting winds, a brisk delight,
Each breath a wonder, bold and bright.
Frost-draped whispers weave through the trees,
Carried on currents of winter breeze.

A realm aglow with winter's spark,
Illuminates shadows in the dark.
Nature's art, a fleeting sight,
In the embrace of luminescent light.

Stars twinkle gently in the sky,
While frostbite dances, ever nigh.
Wrapped in the cool, a stillness reigns,
In the glow of night, serenity gains.

As the dawn approaches, the glow will fade,
But memories linger, softly made.
In every crystal, a story ignites,
Of luminescent frostbite, winter nights.

Ghostly Luminosity

In whispers soft, the shadows wane,
A light emerges from the pain.
Specters dance in silver white,
Glowing gently through the night.

Beneath the stars, the echoes play,
With flickers bright, they weave and sway.
Phantoms drawing near in grace,
A haunting glow, a warm embrace.

Trees are dressed in spectral gleam,
While moonbeams cast a shivering dream.
Lost in this ghostly, tender air,
Ethereal wonders linger there.

Moments stolen from the past,
In twilight's grip, we breathe, we last.
A luminous dance that intertwines,
As light and shadow, fate designs.

Awake, we find the night's refrain,
A ghostly touch that breaks the chain.
With every breath, the seas unfold,
In silent praise, the heart consoled.

Illumination of the Icebound World

In the stillness, ice takes flight,
Reflections gleam, a fragile sight.
Crystals twinkle in cold embrace,
Nature's art, a shimmering grace.

The winds carve tales upon the ground,
Whispers of frost, a haunting sound.
As daylight fades, the colors play,
Illuminating winter's sway.

Glistening paths of shadow stretch,
Beneath the moon, the stars etch.
Each breath a cloud, a fleeting ghost,
In this cold realm, we wander most.

Glimmers dance on frozen lakes,
A tranquil world, where silence wakes.
In icy realms, light flows like streams,
Illumined thoughts, like distant dreams.

As dawn approaches, cold turns warm,
Nature awakens, breaking form.
A fleeting vision, bright and clear,
In the icebound world, we hold dear.

Veil of the Glacial Light

A veil unfolds, a soft caress,
The glacial light, a quiet fest.
Whispers weave through winter's breath,
In this cool realm, we find our rest.

Frosted branches, tales untold,
Under the glow, the night grows bold.
Mirror-like pools reflect the sky,
Where ancient secrets drift and sigh.

The air, so crisp, a sharp embrace,
Each heartbeat echoes through this space.
Shadows linger, stretching thin,
A luminous dance where dreams begin.

Stars alight on coldest nights,
As the world unfolds in soft delights.
Veils of mist, a gentle shroud,
In glacial light, we are endowed.

Within this realm where spirits roam,
We find our way, we feel at home.
Bound by the ice, we drift and sway,
Under the glacial light's soft ray.

Frosted Fragments of the Sky

Frosted fragments, a canvas wide,
Whispers of clouds in moonlit tide.
Fragments shimmering, pale and bright,
Dancing softly in the fading light.

Each star a drop of icy grace,
Scattered visions in time and space.
Rippling mirrors of the night's embrace,
In this quiet, we find our place.

A hush of wind, a breath so chill,
Where hope ignites, and hearts can fill.
The night sky wears a jeweled crown,
In frosted dreams, we won't drown.

As darkness swallows, shadows blend,
Fragments shimmer, the night will mend.
From icy shards, our spirits soar,
Frosted whispers, forevermore.

Illuminate the tales of light,
In every fragment, the soul takes flight.
The sky is ours, a boundless sea,
In frosted beauty, we are free.

Ribbons of Radiance Over the Tundra

In the stillness of the night,
Colors dance, a pure delight.
Silver beams and glimmers bright,
Paint the tundra with their light.

Whispers of the winter's song,
Carry dreams both deep and long.
Through the frost, the night so bold,
Bears the warmth from stories told.

Stars above in velvet skies,
Echo tales of ancient cries.
Each shimmering, a guiding thread,
Leading hearts where hopes are fed.

The frozen ground begins to shine,
As nature weaves her grand design.
Ribbons of light, a timeless chase,
Enchant us with their warm embrace.

In this realm where shadows play,
Night transforms to light of day.
With a touch, the world ignites,
Beneath the tapestries of nights.

The Luminescence of a Winter's Breath

Breath of winter, crisp and clear,
Whispers secrets in the ear.
Softly glowing, mist like snow,
Guides the heart where dreams may go.

In the hush, where silence reigns,
Every heartbeat softly gains.
Frosty edges, glimmers bright,
Line the landscape, pure delight.

Colors blend in harmony,
Painting stillness endlessly.
Shimmering light, a gentle tease,
Bringing forth a sense of ease.

Nature's canvas, cold yet warm,
Holds within a perfect charm.
As we breathe in, we can feel,
Winter's magic, pure and real.

In the glow of moonlit white,
Find the beauty in the night.
The world awaits, with hope anew,
In the winter's breath, so true.

Dreaming in the Cold Luminance

Underneath the starlit sky,
Dreams awaken, drift and fly.
Frozen air within us stirs,
In the stillness, magic purrs.

Luminous flakes like gentle sighs,
Fall like whispers, softly cries.
Each spark dances, swirls around,
Wrapping earth in silver crown.

In this realm of moonbeam glow,
Hearts connect in quiet flow.
Dreams take flight on frosted wings,
In the silence, wonder sings.

Wandering through this frosty maze,
Chasing light in winter's haze.
Echoes of the night unfold,
In the dreams, a tale retold.

Cold luminance guides the way,
Filling souls with light's array.
In this world, we find our peace,
And see our worries gently cease.

Whispers of Light in the Snowy Silence

In the quiet, soft and wide,
Whispers of light begin to glide.
Touch of frost and gentle glow,
Blanket earth in purest snow.

Nights embrace the soft embrace,
Moonlit paths, a gentle trace.
Every flake, a story spun,
Infinite, where dreams are won.

Dancing shadows in moonlight play,
Casting visions, bright as day.
Softly echoing all around,
In this silence, magic found.

Gentle whispers through the trees,
Carried forth on winter's breeze.
Kissed by light, the world awakes,
With each breath, a love that stakes.

In snowy silence, hearts take flight,
Embraced by whispers, soft and light.
In this moment, pure and true,
Find the beauty, wait for you.

Encounters with Ethereal Light

In the hush of twilight's glow,
Soft whispers of dawn begin to flow.
Shadows dance with fleeting grace,
Ethereal light paints every space.

Ghostly forms weave through the air,
Echoes of dreams, both fragile and rare.
Colors blend in a soft embrace,
In this moment, we find our place.

Stars twinkle in the evening's sigh,
As hopes and wishes drift and fly.
Light caresses the earth so bright,
Breathing life into the night.

A shimmer glows through silent trees,
Carried softly on a gentle breeze.
Each encounter, a fleeting spark,
Illuminating the silent dark.

In the depths of the mystic glow,
We wander where our hearts can flow.
Ethereal moments, pure and rare,
Guide us through the midnight air.

Glacial Reflections at Daybreak

Morning breathes on frozen lakes,
Glaciers whisper as daylight wakes.
Mirrors of ice, a world of dreams,
Catching sunlight with shimmering beams.

Crisp air dances with gentle light,
Painting horizons with colors bright.
Each reflection tells a tale anew,
Of ancient glories bathed in blue.

Mountains stand in tranquil pride,
Veils of frost, nature's guide.
In the stillness, secrets confide,
Within the beauty, we abide.

Nature's canvas, a sight to behold,
Silent stories waiting to unfold.
Glacial wonders in morning's hue,
With every heartbeat, a world so true.

As day breaks, shadows retreat,
A symphony where earth and sky meet.
In reflections, we find our fate,
In the glacial glow, we celebrate.

The Gleam of Solitude in Snowdrifts

Beneath the sky, a blanket white,
Snowdrifts glimmer in soft twilight.
Every flake, a frozen tear,
In solitude, we hold you near.

The world hushed, a gentle sigh,
Leaves fall silent as dreams drift by.
Footprints fade in the silver glow,
In quiet moments, secrets grow.

Whispers echo in the chill,
As time slows to perfect still.
Each breath puffs in the frosty air,
In solitude, magic we share.

Snow-laden branches arch and bend,
Nature's beauty without an end.
In the quiet, hearts align,
In the gleam, we truly shine.

A world painted with layers bright,
In solitude, peace takes flight.
Embrace the silence, let it stay,
For in snowdrifts, dreams are laid.

A Symphony of Light in a Subzero Realm

In a realm where the ice meets the sky,
A symphony of light begins to lie.
Notes of frost on a crystal sea,
Creating harmony, wild and free.

Bells of winter chime with grace,
Illuminating every place.
With every shimmer, stories unfold,
Of warmth that defies the bitter cold.

Stars play their tune in the night,
A dance of flares, brilliant and bright.
In the subzero, shadows hum,
With whispers of dreams still to come.

Glowing horizons call us near,
To lose ourselves in winter's sphere.
A symphony that draws us close,
In this chill, we find our dose.

Frosted branches sway and bend,
As every note begins to blend.
In the cold, we find a spark,
In the symphony of light, we embark.

Ethereal Ice

Crystals sparkle in the night,
Whispers cold, a pure delight.
Silent air, the world holds still,
Nature's touch, a frozen thrill.

Moonlight dances on the ground,
In this place, peace can be found.
Every breath a frosty sigh,
Underneath the vast, clear sky.

Snowflakes fall like feathered dreams,
Glistening under gentle beams.
Winter's magic fills the air,
Beauty blooms everywhere.

Icicles hang from trees so high,
Reflecting stars that softly sigh.
Each moment, a jewel's grace,
Trapped within this frozen space.

With each step, the world is new,
Ethereal ice, a wondrous view.
In this stillness, hearts unite,
Wrapped in warmth, out of the night.

Northern Lights Whisper

Dancing colors sweep the sky,
In soft hues, they twist and fly.
Whispers of the cosmic dance,
Inviting all to gaze and trance.

Emerald greens, and violet rays,
In a symphony of cosmic plays.
Each shimmer, a tale untold,
A celestial story in colors bold.

The cold night air begins to hum,
While distant stars flicker and strum.
Underneath the glowing veil,
The world's magic seems to sail.

In the stillness, a heart takes flight,
Captured by the wondrous light.
Nature's brushstroke paints the dark,
With strokes of shimmering spark.

As dawn approaches, colors fade,
Yet memories of wonder stay made.
Whispers linger on the breeze,
A promise of magic, beauty, and peace.

Frosted Dreams

In the morning's gentle glow,
Dreams of winter softly flow.
Fields adorned in icy lace,
Nature's breath, a warm embrace.

Each petal kissed by frosted dew,
The world feels fresh, the sky so blue.
Whispers of a soft, clear night,
Crafting dreams in the morning light.

Snowflakes dance like secrets shared,
Every moment treasured, cared.
Frosted dreams take wing and fly,
Carried gently through the sky.

A canvas white, a breath unmatched,
In this realm, our hearts are attached.
With every step, enchantment grows,
Frosted dreams in gentle flows.

As daylight fades, a hush descends,
In winter's realm, our wonder blends.
Holding close these visions bright,
In frosted dreams, we find our light.

Celestial Reflections

Beneath the stars, the water gleams,
A mirror for our quiet dreams.
Ripples whisper ancient tales,
Carried softly on night gales.

Galaxies twinkle in the deep,
In silence vast, our souls do leap.
Reflected hopes like silver beams,
Guide us through the endless themes.

Moonlit paths on tranquil seas,
Carrying with them the softest pleas.
Each wave a prayer, a wish to soar,
In celestial realms forevermore.

The night's embrace, a comforting shroud,
Where thoughts are free, unbound, and proud.
With every glance up at the dome,
We find the cosmos feels like home.

As dawn creeps up, the magic fades,
Yet in our hearts, its joy cascades.
Celestial reflections still remain,
Whispering their truth in our veins.

Frostbitten Radiance of Distant Stars

In the night's deep hue, they gleam,
Whispers of dreams on silver beams.
Frozen petals fall like tears,
Each glimmer stirring dormant fears.

Beneath the blanket, cold and vast,
Galaxies drift in silence cast.
Hope lingers in their frozen light,
Guiding the way through endless night.

The icy breath of cosmic winds,
Caresses shadows where hope begins.
Stars pulse softly, a quiet guide,
Through the dark where secrets hide.

Each flicker tells of distant screams,
Of fractured worlds and shattered dreams.
Yet in the chill, warmth is found,
In the quiet, love knows no bound.

So gaze above at the endless sky,
Let the frostbitten light draw your sigh.
In every sparkle, a story lies,
A reminder of beauty beneath the ice.

The Color of Cold in a Wintry Embrace

Soft whispers of snow on the ground,
Where silence and peace can be found.
The air is sharp, crisp with delight,
As twilight dances into the night.

Blue shadows stretch across the land,
Under the touch of winter's hand.
Embers of twilight, a dimming glow,
Wrapped in the warmth of a world aglow.

Icicles hang like chandeliers,
Holding the breath of fleeting years.
The trees wear coats of frosty lace,
Cradling time in a cold embrace.

Each flake that falls, a fleeting sigh,
A moment captured, now goodbye.
Yet in this chill, our hearts can rise,
Emboldened by the beauty in the skies.

The color of cold is the warmth within,
A light that flickers, shy to begin.
In winter's realm, magic unfurls,
As love endures through the frozen swirls.

Chasing Dawn in the White Wilderness

In the hush of morning's glow,
Whispers of light begin to flow.
Through the trees, a promise gleams,
Chasing the night from hidden dreams.

Frost-kissed branches sway and sigh,
As the daybreak paints the sky.
Each ray a brush with colors bold,
A canvas unfolding, tales told.

Footprints follow where shadows blend,
Chasing dawn as it beckons, friend.
The wilderness cries in muted tones,
A symphony played on icy bones.

In the heart of splendors white,
Life unfurls with each new light.
A journey begun in the chill of morn,
In the embrace of a world reborn.

As the sun creeps over the land,
The beauty of dawn takes my hand.
In every breath, a new day starts,
Chasing light that warms our hearts.

Shards of Light in a Frozen World

In the depths of winter's grasp,
Light fractures, giving hope a clasp.
Each shard a beacon, bright and rare,
Lit by the sun's gentle care.

Icicles dangle, diamonds in air,
As whispers of warmth begin to flare.
The frost-bitten ground, a shimmering sheet,
Cradles the silence beneath our feet.

When shadows flicker and hope seems thin,
The shards of light pull us from within.
They twinkle softly, a promise made,
That even the cold cannot evade.

Through the frost, the colors dance,
With every twirl, the heart's romance.
In the frozen world, beauty ignites,
Lighting the dark with tender bytes.

So dream in the cold, where stories weave,
In the shards of light, embrace believe.
For even the frost can paint the day,
In hues that chase the chill away.

Radiance in the Land of Frost

In the stillness, whispers play,
Crystals dance, where shadows sway.
The sun breaks through, a gentle light,
Casting warmth on winter's night.

Silent snowflakes, soft and bright,
Blanket earth in purest white.
Each flake wears a crown of gleam,
A fleeting, delicate dream.

Frosted branches, nature's lace,
In this still, enchanted space.
Every breath a cloud of grace,
Time stands still, a gentle pace.

Beneath the moon, a soft embrace,
The night's cool kiss, a tender trace.
Stars awaken, twinkling high,
Magic woven through the sky.

In the dawn's light, shadows fade,
Warmth returns, the frost will wade.
Yet in our hearts, the beauty stays,
Radiance in winter's gaze.

Reflections of a Chilling Majesty

Mountains rise with icy crowns,
Whispers echo through the towns.
Glistening peaks, so bold and bright,
Holding secrets of the night.

Streams of silver glide with grace,
Mirror skies in their embrace.
Underneath the frosty hue,
Nature's beauty, pure and true.

Winds may howl, but still we stand,
In this frozen, fairytale land.
Each breath whispers tales of old,
Of majesty in winter's hold.

Glimmers shine on crystal wings,
As the fragile silence sings.
Chilling beauty, haunting song,
In this realm, we all belong.

So let us chase the fleeting light,
Through the frosts, both day and night.
In reflection, we find our way,
Embracing winter's grand display.

Starlit Crystals in the Chill

Night descends, the world is still,
Crystals glimmer, hearts to fill.
Stars sprinkle magic in the air,
Whispers of dreams linger there.

Underneath a velvet sky,
Frosted echoes softly fly.
Every flake a distant star,
Guiding souls from near and far.

Glistening paths of icy allure,
Draw us close, forever pure.
Moonlight spills like silver wine,
In this realm, all hearts entwine.

Chill of night, a gentle breath,
Sings of life and silent death.
Yet amidst the cold and dark,
Starlit crystals leave their mark.

Embrace the frost, the night's soft grip,
Taste the magic on your lip.
In this stillness, find your thrill,
As starlit crystals shape the chill.

Glacial Glow of Forgotten Times

Through the ages, ice has grown,
Whispers of the past are sown.
Glaciers speak in ancient tongues,
Melodies of old still sung.

Frozen tales in crystal shells,
Every shard, a story tells.
Echoes of a world divine,
In the glacial glow, we find.

Nature's art, a sculptor grand,
Carving moments in the land.
Light dances on the icy streams,
Revealing hidden, timeless dreams.

In the quiet, find the spark,
Of history within the dark.
Footprints left by those before,
Guiding hearts to seek the shore.

So let us wander, hand in hand,
Through this frosty, whispered land.
In the glacial glow, we see,
The forgotten tales that set us free.

Empress of Light in the Frosted Night

In twilight's embrace, she reigns so bright,
Her silver glow dances, a wondrous sight.
Frosted whispers swirl, secrets take flight,
An empress of shadows, veiled in the night.

With starlit grace, she paints the land,
Each glimmer a promise, a magic so grand.
Floating like dreams, a soft, gentle hand,
Holding the cold in a delicate strand.

Moonbeams cry out, the trees gently sway,
Captured in silence, the world turns to gray.
Yet, light spills forth, chasing gloom away,
Life in her glow, an enchanting ballet.

In her presence, the frost comes alive,
Winter's breath stirs, and the night starts to thrive.
With every soft flicker, the shadows arrive,
Empress of night, in her reign we survive.

Glimmers of warmth within shadows she weaves,
As crystals cascade from the boughs of the leaves.
Within the cold night, our heart gently cleaves,
To the empress of light, in her grace, we believe.

Enchanted Light on Snowy Peaks

Above the world where the snowflakes gleam,
Enchanted hues burst forth, a vivid dream.
Light filters softly, like whispers that seam,
On snowy peaks, where the lost find their theme.

Mountains adorned in a crystal embrace,
Each gust of wind leaves a delicate trace.
Golden horizons begin to efface,
The shadows of winter that tempers the space.

Beneath the sky, where the eagles take flight,
The sun spills its magic, igniting the night.
In valleys of peace, hearts dance in delight,
On those snowy peaks, all wrong turns to right.

In the stillness, a symphony plays,
Of soft echoes, lost in the white haze.
A world enchanted, like ancient displays,
Awakening dreams in the winter's arrays.

With every moment, the light weaves its sway,
A canvas of wonders, both bold and fey.
On snowy peaks where the heart finds its way,
The enchanted light leads us, come what may.

The Dance of Indigo and Ice

Under the heavens, where colors collide,
Indigo whispers, and icy winds slide.
A ballet of hues, in the frost they abide,
Nature's own canvas, where dreams won't hide.

Twilight embraces the firmament's face,
Each movement glistens with delicate grace.
Shadows entwine in a silvery space,
The dance of the night, a mystical chase.

Crystals like stars weave a story untold,
In the chill of the air, their brilliance unfolds.
Artistry spins in the icy cold gold,
While indigo fades, a beauty to hold.

The world is alive in this frigid ballet,
Where ice forms a stage, and shadows at play.
Emotions unearthing the night from the gray,
In the dance of indigo, we dream and sway.

As dawn breaks the silence with pastel delight,
The echoes of midnight take gentle flight.
With each fading whisper, the day greets the night,
In the dance of the colors, we find pure light.

Whispering Winds of the Cold Blaze

Through branches that tremble, whispers do weave,
A tale of the winds, on frosty eves.
Their voice, a soft song, as night takes its leave,
In the cold blaze of winter, the heart believes.

In chilling gusts, a secret unfolds,
The breath of the mountains, in tales never told.
With every soft rustle, an invitation bold,
To dance with the frost, in magic untold.

Frozen horizons gleam under the moon,
A symphony stirs, a hauntingly tune.
While whispering winds carve the silvered dunes,
The essence of winter, a mystical boon.

Carried on breezes, soft memories flow,
Of laughter and warmth, where no shadows go.
In this cold blaze, where the heart starts to glow,
We find our own rhythm, wherever winds blow.

So let us embrace the soft howls of night,
With hearts intertwined, our spirits take flight.
For in whispering winds, we discover our light,
In the cold blaze of winter, our dreams ignite.

The Gleam of Winter's Veil

Silvery whispers in the breeze,
Snowflakes twirl like ancient leaves.
Blanket soft on earth's embrace,
Quiet stillness, a perfect space.

Moonlight glimmers on the frost,
Nature's beauty, never lost.
Each branch draped in a crystal gown,
Winter's breath, a silent crown.

Footprints shallow in the snow,
Where echoes of the cold winds blow.
Stars above, like diamonds shine,
In the dark, their light divine.

A world adorned in shades of gray,
Yet warmth lingers in the day.
Fires crackle, stories weave,
In winter's tale, we all believe.

Spring will come, a distant thought,
But now in winter, calm is sought.
Let the chill dance in our veins,
Embrace the hush, the gentle rains.

Aurora's Dance Upon the Ice

Colors burst in frozen skies,
Nature's magic captivates the eyes.
Greens and pinks in swirling grace,
The aurora paints a serene face.

Beneath a dome of shimmering light,
The world stands still in awe of sight.
Ice reflects each brilliant hue,
A cosmic show, just for the few.

Chill winds wrap like a gentle shawl,
As night creates a stunning call.
Dancing shadows in the glow,
Whisper secrets from below.

Silence reigns, yet hearts ignite,
Magic pulses in the night.
Each moment holds a breath of peace,
In this stillness, worries cease.

The icy ground adorned with dreams,
As nature shares her vibrant schemes.
Underneath the sky's embrace,
A perfect moment finds its place.

Frosted Dreams in the Midnight Sun

When twilight falls in winter's hold,
A tale of warmth yet to be told.
Shadows stretch across the field,
In frosted dreams, our hopes are healed.

The sun dips low, a gentle sigh,
A golden rim 'neath endless sky.
Each breath of chill ignites the air,
In whispered wishes, we find care.

Frozen whispers on the ground,
Joyful echoes all around.
Life's embrace in frosted light,
Midnight sun makes spirits bright.

Creating paths through snow's expanse,
We walk together, hearts in dance.
In frozen realms, our dreams take flight,
Underneath the stars so bright.

Each moment soft, a fleeting song,
Where visions linger, warm and strong.
Amidst the cold, we search for bliss,
In our dreams, we find our kiss.

Luminous Shadows on Glacial Fields

As daylight fades, the shadows grow,
On glacial fields where streams of glow.
Each crevice holds a story told,
In whispered tones of ice and cold.

Luminous paths through sparkling white,
Guide us gently into night.
The stillness sings a timeless tune,
Beneath the watchful, silver moon.

Frosted whispers in the air,
Each step echoes a silent prayer.
Shadows link like timeless friends,
In winter's grasp, the magic bends.

Beneath our feet, the glimmers spread,
As starlit dreams dance overhead.
In frozen realms, our spirits roam,
Together, we find our way back home.

In whispered winds, the secrets weave,
Luminous shadows, we believe.
Upon the ice, our hopes unite,
In glacial fields, we find the light.

Aurora's Embrace

Colors burst in the night sky,
Whispers of light softly sigh.
Dancing hues of pink and gold,
Nature's secrets, slowly unfold.

Stars blend with the morning glow,
Dreams take flight, gently flow.
A canvas painted with delight,
Aurora's embrace, pure and bright.

In silent wonder, we stand still,
Hearts in sync with the quiet thrill.
Moments captured, forever bound,
In this magic, solace found.

The chill wraps close, but warm we feel,
In nature's art, the world does heal.
Under skies that shift and turn,
For life's beauty, we shall yearn.

With the dawn, the colors fade,
But in our hearts, the light has stayed.
An echo of this mystic plight,
Aurora's embrace, a pure delight.

Chasing Frostfire

In the dark, a flicker bright,
Chasing shadows, a dance of light.
Frosted air, a cool caress,
Igniting souls, a warm excess.

Sparkling flakes, a shimmering race,
Captured in the night's embrace.
We run wild, as dreams ignite,
Chasing frostfire, bold and bright.

Echoes call from far away,
In the chill, we choose to stay.
Every heartbeat, a whispered song,
Together, we find where we belong.

With every spark, our hopes unwind,
In this journey, the heart decides.
A fleeting glimpse of what we seek,
Chasing frostfire, bright and meek.

Through the silence, laughter flows,
In frozen realms, our bond grows.
As morning glimmers, shadows flee,
Chasing frostfire, wild and free.

The Dance of Cold Radiance

Beneath the moon's soft silver glow,
Whispers of winter, breath of snow.
Stars awaken, twinkle and prance,
The universe joins in a waltzing dance.

Frosted branches sway and bend,
Nature's rhythm, no need to pretend.
In the stillness, magic reigns,
Cold radiance flows through our veins.

Each flake a story, unique and rare,
In this ballet, we become aware.
With every twist and every turn,
The heart ignites, the soul does burn.

Footprints trace a pathway bright,
Guided by stars, through the night.
The dance unfolds, and moments freeze,
In the thrill of winter's timeless tease.

As dawn approaches, shadows wane,
Yet the echoes of our dance remain.
Embers of joy, with every glance,
We become part of the frozen dance.

Twilight in the Frozen Realm

Twilight drapes the land in blue,
A frozen world, quiet and true.
Glistening icicles catch the light,
Whispers of day fade into night.

The horizon blurs, dreams take flight,
In this moment, hearts feel light.
Snowflakes twinkle like stars above,
Wrapped in winter's gentle love.

Silhouettes of trees stand tall,
Beneath the twilight's tender call.
A blanket of silence, soft and deep,
In this frozen realm, secrets keep.

As shadows stretch and time stands still,
The beauty of dusk, we long to fill.
With every breath, the world weaves tight,
Twilight's grasp, a soft delight.

In the hush, a promise gleams,
Echoes of hope fill our dreams.
As day gives way to night's soft helm,
We find our peace in the frozen realm.

Dreaming in Crystal

In the quiet of night, dreams ignite,
Whispers of wishes, taking flight.
Stars drape the sky, soft and bright,
Magic unfolds in silvery light.

Through the window, visions cascade,
Glowing paths of the dreams we've made.
Hope dances gently, unafraid,
In crystal realms, where memories fade.

Each breath a promise, tender and clear,
In this dreamscape, we draw near.
Voices of laughter, we hold dear,
Woven in starlight, year by year.

Underneath the moon's gentle gaze,
Every heartbeat sings, a delicate phrase.
Together we wander through this maze,
In dream's embrace, forever we blaze.

A tapestry spun of silken threads,
Where hopes are born, and darkness sheds.
In crystal realms, our spirit spreads,
Awake in wonder, where magic leads.

Glittering Echoes from the Glacial Edge

On the glacial edge where silence sings,
Echoes dance, with the joy winter brings.
Icicles shimmer, catching the light,
A frozen world, bathed in white.

Beneath the surface, the secrets lie,
Whispers of frost, under the sky.
Each flake a story, a moment in time,
Echoes of laughter, a silent rhyme.

The crisp air lingers, biting and clear,
While shadows of twilight draw near.
Each glimmering sound a reminder dear,
Of winter's breath, we hold near.

In the stillness, our hearts align,
As the stars above begin to twine.
Glittering echoes, a sign divine,
From the glacial edge, our souls entwine.

With every shimmer, the magic grows,
In the land of ice, where the cold wind blows.
A bond unbroken, the warmth we chose,
Glittering echoes where love bestows.

Winter's Ancient Canvas

Upon the ground, a canvas old,
Winter paints in shades of gold.
With brush of frost, the world transforms,
In silence deep, where beauty warms.

Each flake unique, a fleeting dream,
Nature's art, a gentle gleam.
Footprints linger, paths rewind,
Stories written, intertwined.

Pine trees wear their coats of white,
Underneath the starry night.
Whispers echo through the trees,
As winter's breath brings forth the freeze.

A gentle hush blankets the land,
As nature's pulse takes a stand.
With every brushstroke hand in hand,
Winter's magic, ever so grand.

The moonlight spills, a silver hue,
Across a canvas vast and true.
In winter's grasp, all things renew,
An ancient tale, forever cue.

We walk upon this frozen art,
In every moment, a brand new start.
Winter's canvas, pure as the heart,
A quiet song, each note a part.

Frozen Skies

Underneath the frozen skies,
Winter's breath, a soft disguise.
Clouds like blankets, white and grey,
Hiding warmth, keeping light at bay.

Stars like diamonds, piercing through,
Guiding hearts, shining anew.
Each twinkle whispers, tales of old,
Stories woven in threads of gold.

As night unfolds, the silence grows,
Fragrant winds of winter blows.
With every chill, a promise keeps,
In frozen skies, our spirit leaps.

Moonlight dances, casting glow,
Over the land, where shadows flow.
In the vast expanse, dreams bestow,
Frozen skies, where spirits sow.

Together, we gaze, hearts aligned,
In the stillness, love defined.
Through the frost, our hopes refined,
Under frozen skies, all combined.

Brilliant Eyes

In a world of white, your gaze ignites,
Brilliant eyes like starry nights.
Mirrors of dreams, so pure and bright,
Guiding me through the fading light.

Each glance a spark, a hidden flame,
Calling my soul, whispering your name.
Together we wander, the world so tame,
In the winter's chill, we play the same game.

With laughter like bells, echoing clear,
You warm the silence, drawing me near.
In your brilliant eyes, I find my cheer,
Reflecting the wonders we hold dear.

When snowflakes fall and shadows blend,
Brilliant eyes, our hearts transcend.
Every moment, a heart to mend,
In the glow of love that has no end.

As the world drifts in quiet delight,
Together we chase the waning light.
With every gaze, the future is bright,
In your brilliant eyes, we take flight.

Shimmering Glaciation

In icy realms where silence speaks,
The crystals dance, their beauty peaks.
Each flake a gem, a story spun,
Beneath the vast and shining sun.

Mountains clad in azure hue,
Reflecting light, an endless view.
The air is crisp, the world stands still,
In glaciation's wonder, hearts fulfill.

Rivers frozen, a glassy flow,
Underneath, the secrets glow.
Nature's art in vibrant blue,
A silent song, a world anew.

Animals roam in quiet grace,
Footprints mark each hidden place.
While shadows cast by twilight's kiss,
Embrace the night in tranquil bliss.

The cosmos shines with jeweled light,
As day gives way to starry night.
In shimmering glaciation's arms,
We find our peace, our deepest charms.

Luminous Polar Nights

In stillness deep, the hours glide,
As polar nights, in shadows, bide.
The auroras dance, a vibrant show,
In fleeting hues of greenish glow.

Stars twinkle bright in velvet skies,
Under the moon's watchful eyes.
Whispers of wind tell tales untold,
Of ancient lands and dreams of old.

A world at rest, where time stands still,
The heartbeats echo, gently thrill.
With every breath, the cold embrace,
Surrounds the night, a warm solace.

Footprints mark the snowy ground,
In solitude, the lost are found.
The hush of night, a tender quilt,
In every flake, a dream is built.

Time drifts soft, like falling snow,
In luminous polar nights aglow.
The world transformed, a dreamlike sight,
Where mysteries dwell in endless night.

Radiance of the Tundra

Beneath the sun's enchanting rays,
The tundra blooms in wild displays.
With colors bright, the earth awakes,
A tapestry that life remakes.

Golden grasses sway in gentle breeze,
Whispers of life among the trees.
The fragile blooms, in joy they sway,
Convert the dusk of fading day.

In harmony, the creatures play,
Underneath the sun's vast sway.
From every nook, a laugh, a sound,
The magic of this land profound.

Frosty mornings greet the dawn,
As shadows dance on emerald lawn.
Each dew drop glistens in the light,
A glimpse of heaven, pure delight.

Radiant hues reflect the day,
In every heart, they find their way.
Through tundra's charm and secret grace,
We learn to hold our rightful place.

Frost-Embroidered Silence

In winter's hold, the world stands still,
A frost-embroidered, silent thrill.
The air so crisp, the silence deep,
In nature's arms, we drift to sleep.

Each flake a whisper, soft as breath,
Marks of beauty, traces of death.
Every branch clothed in icy lace,
Crafted carefully, a frozen grace.

The world transformed, a dreamlike sight,
In muted tones of silver white.
Each step we take, a gentle sound,
In frosted dreams, our hearts unbound.

Night falls soft with stars so bright,
A tapestry of endless light.
In the shadows, truths reside,
In frost-embroidered silence, we confide.

As dawn approaches, colors bloom,
In gradients that chase away gloom.
With every breath, the world awakes,
In winter's arms, a hope remakes.

www.ingramcontent.com/pod-product-compliance
Ingram Content Group UK Ltd.
Pitfield, Milton Keynes, MK11 3LW, UK
UKHW031957131224
452403UK00010B/495